Bella

Brina

By Birdie Chesson
Miss Birdie's Books, Inc.

ISBN:
 978-0-999-28371-4
Copyright 2014 by Birdie Chesson

Table of Contents

One   Big Bones   5

Two   Miss Mina   11

Three   Myles   15

Four   The Party   27

Five   The Aftermath   40

Six   Pageant Day   55

Seven   Grandpop's Heart   60

Eight   Talent Show   64

**To You
Loving <u>You</u>.**

Chapter One
Big Bones

In the distance, I hear a female voice yelling, "Hey Big Bones!"

Then I hear laughter. The voice calling is getting closer. "Big Bones, Slow down!"

Problem is, I know that person is talking about *me*. My cousin Yetta has always had words and phrases to describe me. As I was growing up, I was considered, "*solid*", "*chunky*", "*chubby*" and now it's, "*Big Bones*." I hate all of it.

Yetta finally catches up.
"Brina! You didn't hear me call you?"

"Yeah, I heard you." I said, turning my head, now giving her *the eye*, "Big Bones isn't my name!"

Yetta's eyes got big. "Well, excuse me, Miss Brina!"

"That's better! Now, what do you want?"
"All I was going to say was, you move fast for a *BIG BONE*!" She screams as she runs away.

"I'm gonna get you, Yetta!"
I can't believe I fell for that one again.

My name is Bella. Well, Brina. Ok, it's Sabrina. My mom Charlene named me after a girl in a movie she saw and liked it. But she always called me Bella because she said that I was so beautiful to her. She was such a wonderful woman. I'm constantly trying to remember her because I don't want to ever forget her. I'm glad that when I look in the mirror, I can still see her smile.

She died a few years ago. It was so sudden. One day, she was with me, the next morning I was on my way to New Jersey to live with my Grandpop.

Sometimes, I hate it here, I guess because it still doesn't feel like home. Don't get me wrong, Grandpop takes care of me, but when Yetta calls me names, he doesn't stop her. He makes me eat salads and chicken with no skin. *Who eats chicken with no skin?* He says he wants me healthy but I know it's because he agrees with Yetta. They both say I'm fat. But I don't feel fat. My mom used to always say how beautiful I was and when I was a baby, she used to say I was a juicy girl. That used to make me smile.

But the hardest for me to be here is being called anything other than Bella Brina. When I heard my name I felt so beautiful and loved. No one calls me that since my mom passed away.

I hate school so far because the kids are mean sometimes. The only thing that makes living here bearable is my friends, Belinda and Jasper. Yetta is OK when she wants to be, but sometimes she's mean for no reason. I'm so glad that she's in a different school and not in school with me. She'd have everyone calling me "Big Bones".

I'm from Jacksonville, North Carolina. Life was so much simpler as I remember it. It was just my mom and I, so we did everything together. We even played with my dolls together. Our favorite times were when my mother and I cooked.

Where I'm from, it's OK to have a little meat on your bones. I guess that it's not OK up here. It's embarrassing sometimes, when Grandpop watches what I eat like a hawk. Then I have to eat different things than him and Yetta.

Fried chicken is my favorite. My mom also made the best collard greens, cabbage, candied yams, potato salad, macaroni salad, pork chops, pork ribs, peach cobbler, apple pies; OH MAN! It was only she and I so we used to stuff ourselves crazy with that good stuff. But I can't have any of that anymore and nowadays the greens and the yams are steamed.

Grandpop refuses to let me have any of that. He wants me to lose weight but it's so hard. Maybe I am just *big boned* like they say. I don't know. But Mommy never made me feel bad about myself like Grandpop and Yetta does.

If he sees me sitting on the couch, he always tells me to get me to go outside and play but sometimes I just want to stay in, read or watch television.

School? I hate school. The kids in school are just as mean. Some of the kids heard Yetta call me Big Bones last summer and now they scream it, especially this girl Penny. But at least I do have friends, Jasper and Belinda. I met Belinda one day when I first came here. Some of the kids were making fun of me on the playground and she stood up for me. Jasper is her older cousin and he hangs with us most of the time. We just chill out because we're too old for little kid games and playing with toys. It's great to have friends so I'm not as lonely as I used to be.

The kids in school still whisper behind my back and call me fat. I'm so glad that my mom showed me how beautiful I am, so the things that other people say and do don't bother me... that much.

Chapter Two
Miss Mina

I'll never forget the first time I saw Miss Mina. I had to do a double take because I thought I saw my Mama. She looked like magic. So beautiful, sparkly and shiny. She literally looked like a star.

I've met Miss Mina in my mind a hundred times. She was this gorgeous woman that had a different look everyday. Hair straight, hair curly. She dressed like a rainbow one day, then the next day in all white with diamonds and dressed in all gold with glitter at night. She was... beautiful and different. And when she walked out of the house she always left everyone speechless. But in a good way.

One day, she was sitting on her porch and saw Yetta teasing me. "*BIG BONE, BIG BONE*!" Yetta screamed.

Miss Mina shouted to me, "Hey Pretty girl!"

"Who, me?" I asked.

"Of course you, Sweetheart!" She said with the sweetest southern accent.

That's when I thought I saw my mom. She had a glimmer in her eyes and a bright smile. And when she stood up, she looked like a figure eight. Her curves were perfectly round and for the first time in a long time, I saw myself.

"Come here, Sugar!" she shouted. Jetta just stood there with her jaw dropped as I walked to her. When I walked over, she said,

"You gotta stand up for yourself, Sugar. What's your name?"

"Sabrina. Um, I mean Brina. Well, my mom called me Bella."

"Beautiful."

"Ma'am?"

"Bella means Beautiful. Didn't you know that?"

"I never thought about it, Ma'am."

"Well, you are beautiful and you shouldn't forget it. And you shouldn't let people treat you that way. You Mr. Frank's granddaughter right?"

"Yes, Ma'am."

"Oh Honey, don't call me Ma'am. Makes me feel old. My name is Mina."

Brina, still in awe, "Are you a model? You're so extravagant!"

Mina laughs aloud.

"Extravagant? I love it! I'll have to add that to my introduction. Yes, I am a model, a singer and I do pageants."

"You're really beautiful, Miss Mina."

 "You are such a sweetheart. Thank you, Honey. And I just want you to remember how beautiful you are, Bella Brina."

"Yes, Miss Mina. I will."
Mina went into her house as I walked away towards Yetta, who was still stunned.

"What did she say, Brina?"

"To get you back for calling me Big Bones!"
I pushed Yetta and ran.

Chapter Three
Myles

"**H**e's soooo handsome!" I said to Belinda.

Myles Taylor. He's a little older than me but he has the most pretty eyes I've ever seen on a boy. They're gray with the longest eyelashes.

"And he has such a great smile, Brina!" Belinda whispered. "WAIT! Did he just smile at you? Oh my goodness! He's walking right to us!"

I was stunned. Myles walked right up to us and when he spoke, I melted.
"Sabrina, right? We're in the same math class."

"Yes. That's me." I tried to play it cool.

"Well, I want to invite you and your friends to my party."
"Me?"

"Of course you, Silly. It's in 3 weeks from Saturday." He hands us flyers. "I also wanted to ask what you were doing after school today."

"Me?" I stood there still in shock.

Belinda jumped in. "Nothing! She's doing nothing after school!

I snapped out of it. "Yes. I'm free. Why?"

"Well, I figured that I'd walk you home. We can get to know each other. Do you want to?"

"Ok, Sure."

"Meet me by the library when the final bell rings and we'll walk together."

"She'll be there!" shouted Belinda.
Sure enough when the bell rang, he was there, right on time.

We started walking slowly and he reached for my backpack.

"Can I hold your bag for you?" Impressed, I handed the bag to him. "So you live with your grandfather?" he continued.

"Yeah, and my cousin, Yetta."

"Is that your only family here?"

"Yes. Why do you ask?"

"You don't seem to be from around here. You're different from the other girls. And you have an accent."

"How am I different from the other girls?"

"You have a glow about you. You seem so sure about yourself."

"I am. Don't want to sound conceited but I just love myself. I know that I'm a juicy girl, but it's just another thing that I love about myself. That's what my mom always put in me."

"What happened to her?"

"She died when I was younger and then I came here from Jacksonville to live with my Grandpop." There was a short silence until we got home. "Well, here's my house."

"This has been great, Sabrina." Myles said nervously as he handed me my bag. "I really liked this walk. Can we do it again tomorrow?"

"Sure. I liked the walk too." I watched Myles walk away with a smile.

"Hey Bella." Mina said.

I jumped. "Hi Miss Mina."

"Cute boy. You gotta look out for *them*."

"MINA!" A man shouts. "GET IN HERE!"

Miss Mina's eyes roll. "Speaking of cute boys. See you later, Sweetheart."

When the screen door slammed, I heard more shouting from him and then it was eerily quiet. It was odd but I didn't pay it any mind.

The next day at school, Belinda grabbed my arm excitedly. "So, how was it?"

"What?"

"The walk with Myles."

"It was Ok."

"Ok? Myles is talking all about you! I think he really likes you." Jasper walked up to us. "Oh please! It wasn't all that, Belinda."

"Stop being a hater, Jasper! So tell us about it, Brina."

"Well, I didn't want to brag about it but... it was great! He was such a nice guy. He held my bag and we talked. It was so cool he wants to walk me home again today."

Belinda's face changed. "Did you forget? You said that you'd be there for my audition."

"I'm so sorry. I did forget. I'll ask him to meet me after or just do it tomorrow."

"Tomorrow? That's tryouts for both of us, Brina! You can't be forgetting your friends following some boy!"

"Damn Belinda. Now, who's being a hater? You were the one that set it up in the first place! Whatever. I *said* I'll see what I can do."

Belinda rolls her eyes. "Forget it. Jasper, you going?"

"Sure, I'll be there." Jasper turns to Brina. "Just be careful, Brina. Myles is kind of a player."

"I think that I can handle myself, Jasper. But thanks."

When the final bell rang, Myles was right there. I smiled and we walked home together again. When we got to my porch, this time, he gave me a kiss on the cheek.

"What was that for?" I asked.

Myles smiled. "You're sweet, Sabrina. I really like you."

"OOOOOH I'M TELLING!" Screamed Yetta. "I'M TELLING GRANDPOP!"

"I gotta go."

"Tomorrow?" Myles shouts as he backs up. "I can't. I have tryouts."

"I can wait for you."

"That would be nice." I smile.

Grandpop swung the screen door open. "Brina! Bring your fast ass here!"

Myles started to walk away quickly.

"Young man?"

"Yes Sir?" Myles whispered.

"Don't be coming around here! Brina is too young to be fooling around!"

"Yessir." Myles starts to walk away. I was so embarrassed.

"I wasn't fooling around, Grandpop."

"Oh yeah? Yetta told me you were out here kissing!"

"He just kissed my cheek, Grandpop."

"Listen, it's bad enough I gotta raise you two girls but to raise a great-grand? HELL NO!"

"Grandpop, I'm not going to do that."

"Good. And I don't want you seeing that boy anymore. Something about him I don't like."

"What's wrong with him?"

"Pretty boys like him don't go with big girls."

What Grandpop said, made me mad.
"Big girls? There's nothing wrong with me, Grandpop! Nothing!" I said as I ran into the house.

"Yeah? Well you just better not bring home no babies or you'll both be outta here!" Grandpop shouted.

I write in my diary. *"Grandpop is so unfair. I really like Myles and he likes me. I'm tired of him always on me about my weight. I wish that he would stop."*

The next day, I saw Belinda. She rolled her eyes at me. I walked up to her.

"Sorry I missed your audition yesterday. I didn't really want to."

"It's Ok. You made your choice. I'm sorry I made you feel bad about it. I just don't want you to get a boyfriend and forget about me."

"I won't, Belinda. We're still tight like glue. Best friends, right?"

"Yeah."
After a brief silence, "Well, I bombed anyway."

"What happened?"

"I was singing…"

"Wait singing? Belinda, you don't sing!" I started to laugh. Belinda started to laugh too. "Yeah. And they stopped me mid-song!"

"I thought you were going to dance."

" I changed my mind. Wish I did dance. You should audition, Brina."

"I'll think about it. I don't really like being onstage."

"*You're* such a good singer though."

"Besides around you or at home, I haven't really sang since my Mama's funeral."

"Well, you should try again. Your voice is real pretty."

"Thanks Belinda. New news, my Grandpop told me that I can't see Myles anymore."

"What happened?"

"Yetta told him we were kissing and…"

Belinda's eyes widened. "Kissing? Tell me the details!"

"Nothing happened. When we got to my porch, he kissed my cheek. Yetta saw and told Grandpop and now I can't see him anymore."

"Well, there's ways around that."

"I don't like sneaking around, Belinda."

"It's not really sneaking around. He's just walking you home. It's not like he's your boyfriend yet."

"I think that may be coming soon. I really like him, Belinda. Grandpop probably scared him off though."

Belinda looks off in the distance.
"I don't think so. Look."

Myles is standing next to him locker with his eyes fixed on me.

"Go see what he wants. I think you're right. He might be your boyfriend soon."
We both giggle as I walk away towards Myles.

He waited for me after tryouts that day and walked me home everyday after that.

Chapter Four
The Party

I plop on the bed and stare at the computer screen at Belinda. "I still don't know what to wear tonight!"

"Relax, just wear a cute top and a pair of leggings or the blue dress. It's not like anything ever looks bad on you. You're just the right kind of curvy." We both snicker.

"Ok. That dress does look nice on me. Hugs me just right."

"You know, It's like you'll be the hostess at this party."

"Didn't think of it that way till you just said it. He *is* kinda like my man."

"Kinda? Didn't he ask you yet?"

"Not yet, I think he might tonight."

"Oh, I thought he did. All of the kids are talking about y'all. Even Jasper told me that Myles mentioned you in the boys' locker room. I thought he asked you already."

"I would've told you, Belinda. I tell you everything."

"I don't know. I figured everyone has secrets."

"Oh yeah? What are you hiding from *me*, Belinda?"

"Oh my life isn't juicy *yet*! So I ain't got nothing to hide *yet*."

"Well, I won't be hiding anything. What are *you* wearing?"

"Cute top and leggings." Both girls laugh.

"Looks like we got our outfits. Get dressed and come over so we can get dolled up. Then we'll call the car service to the party."

"Ok. Grandpop knows I'm spending the night with you so I'm all good over here."

"Alright. See you here around 6."

"Cool." The screen goes black and I turn off the computer.

I hurried up, taking my shower and got dressed. As I pack my bag, I grab the blue dress and left the house. As I close the screen door, I hear a light voice.

"Hey Sweetheart, where are you rushing to?"

"A party." I said, shyly.

"Nice, that cute boy going to be there?"

"It's *his* party."

"*Real nice.* Oh wait, I have something for you."

Miss Mina went into her house and quickly came back out. She hands me a small gift bag. "I've been meaning to give this to you since I saw you last."

I look in the bag. A bright red lipstick, perfume and a note.

"Why me?

"Why not you? You deserve to feel pretty. I hope you don't mind."

I notice a bandage on her wrist.
"What happened to your wrist?"

I fell cleaning. I'm clumsy that way."

"Oh. Yeah, I'm clumsy too." I said, cautiously.

"The paper in the bag is an event I never tried out before. You can ask your grandfather if you can participate. I'm a performer but this one is like a…"

Looking at the paper, "A mother-daughter pageant." I finished. "Wow. I don't know about this."

"I know… well, don't rush to any decisions. I just wanted to try something new in my pageantry. You're a pretty girl and you can sorta pass for my daughter… It's $1,000 each if we win, and I know we both can use the money."

Excitedly, I said, " A thousand dollars? Yeah, we do!"

We both laugh. "Just think about it, Bella. If you're interested, just come by next Tuesday and we can start practicing."

"Ok." I was so excited, I almost skipped away.

"Enjoy your party!" Mina shouts.

"Thanks, I will. And thanks for the stuff. I'll wear the lipstick tonight."

"You go, Girl!"

I walk to Belinda's house. Belinda opens the door and we run upstairs. I pull out the lipstick and start to put it on.

"Ooooh Girl! I'm *loving* that lipstick! Where did you get it?"

"My neighbor, Miss Mina." As I pucker.

"The model? Yeah she's pretty and all, but I heard my mom say that Mr. Don beats her ass."

"I don't think so. I think that I would have heard something by now."

"Whatever. You ready?"
I pop out my lips and step back from the mirror. "I love it. What do *you* think, Belinda?"

"I think you're gonna have a boyfriend by the end of the night!"

We get to the party, Myles walks up to us and hands us cups.

I take a gulp and instantly almost choked. "What is this? I almost spit it out!"

"It's jungle juice! I made it myself. Have a seat or hit the dance floor! I'll be with you in a minute!" He yells over the crowd as he walks away.

"This jungle juice is good!" yells Belinda.

"Yeah. Kinda weird but I like it. There's a lot of people here." I yelled.

"Oh there's Jasper and Penny, I'm gonna say hi. I'll be right back."

"Penny? I thought you didn't like her."

"I don't. But her and Jasper is calling me over." Belinda winks. I sit down on the couch and take another sip. I look over in their direction but they're not there anymore. I get up so fast my head rushed. "Oh man." I said to myself. "I better take it easy." I walk to the door.

"There you are!" Myles grabs my arm. "Let's go upstairs." I look up for Belinda and Jasper but I still can't find them.

I pull away from Myles. "I gotta find Belinda."

"Her and Jas just left with Penny. I just saw them."

"No they wouldn't just leave me."

"Belinda told me that she's putting you in good hands. Just c'mon. We'll be right back downstairs, Sabrina. I've gotta tell you something." He smiles.

"Fine. But we'll be right back."
He leads me up the stairs into a room and the door closes behind us.

" Is this your room?"

"Nah. This is my parent's room. Just wanted to show you something."

My head rushed again. "Was something in that juice? I feel funny."

"Yours had some of my *secret* sauce." Myles said slyly wiggling his head. "Just chill Sabrina.

You'll get used to it. Take off your shoes. Get comfortable."

He takes off my shoes. "You have pretty feet, Sabrina." He kisses my leg.

My head starts to spin. " I don't feel good, Myles."

"Just lay back." Myles puts on music. He turns up the volume.

"Turn the music down, Myles. My head is spinning."

Myles turns off the lights. I feel the bed move. I feel his hands under my dress. He abruptly pulls my panties off and glides his hands up my legs. "Do you like this, Sabrina?"

"No, Myles. I don't like this. Please stop."

"Come on, Sabrina. Don't be a tease. You want to be my girlfriend, right?" Myles turns the music up louder.

"Yes. I mean no, not like this. I want to go *now*."

He puts my hand down his pants. I snatch my hand back and push him away. He pulls my leg up and sticks his finger inside of me. I kick him off the bed with the other leg.

"Myles! What the hell are you doing?" I stand up too fast and I hit the floor. "I can't feel my legs! I can't see. Turn the lights ON!" I scream.

He turns the lights on. "Why can't you just relax, Sabrina?" He stands there exposed from the waist down.

"You know, I thought you were cooler than this. I thought you wanted to be my girlfriend." He kisses my cheek and rubs my shoulders. He steps back, standing up straight, now holding his penis.

I start to cry. "I just don't know what's going on, Myles. I feel so confused. I thought you liked me."

He grabs my face; "You think that I'd have you up here if I didn't want you? I could do you right here, right now, piss on you when I'm finished with you and I'd *still* be doing you a favor." He slaps my face with his penis.

He stands up and zips his pants up. "Listen, nobody wanted to talk to you because you're fat. But I said to myself, *give her a chance,* because you have a cute face and confidence. You seemed kind of cool. But you're just a dick tease. Forget you, bitch. I've got other options." Myles laughs and leaves.

Still crying with my head spinning, I get my bearings and put on my shoes. I try to walk but my legs feel like jelly and I can't find my underwear.

I don't even know how much time has passed but I slowly get up and walk out of the room. On my way down the stairs, I see my panties in Myles' hands, as he's talking loud to a crowd of people. He doesn't see me so I slip out of the house quietly. I want to start walking to Belinda's house but I know it's too far. I'm trying so hard to register what just happened. I can't even imagine what could've or would've happened. I don't even know what time it is.

I just start walking.

Feels like I've been walking forever when I see Miss Mina coming out of a club. I start crying again. "Miss Mina!" I cried out. I start stumbling towards her.

"Hey Bella." Her smile disappears. "What's wrong? What happened?"

"Please take me with you."

"Sure, Sugar." She said worriedly.

I get in her car. I put on my seatbelt and fell asleep. When we get to the house, I quietly slip in and run upstairs. I take my dress off and through it in the trash.

Staring in the mirror at myself, Myles voice echoes in my head. "Stupid Bitch." "Nobody wants you because you're fat."

"What the hell was I thinking?" I shake it off and go take a hot shower and get into bed.

I doze off for what feels like a few minutes and I jump up to the sun beaming in my face. I look at my clock. "Crap!" I'm gonna be late to school. I grab a pair of jeans, a tee shirt, my book bag and start running down the stairs. Grandpop yells. "I thought you were at your friend's house last night."

"YYeah." I stammer. "I forgot my book bag." I blurted.

"Well, hurry up!" Looking at his watch. "You're already late!"

Chapter Five
The Aftermath

"**W**here the hell were you?" screamed Belinda.

"I had to go home." I whispered. I closed my locker.

"I heard where you went." Jasper said, sarcastically.

"I heard too. But I want to hear it from *you*."

"I don't want to talk about it, Belinda. Definitely not right now."

I see Myles in the distance with the football team and Penny, laughing.

"Where were you guys? You left me." I say tearfully.

"You go off and get your wax on, wax off with Myles and you're asking *us*, where *we* were?" said Jasper.

"Yeah, Penny told us you left." Belinda interjects.

"I looked for you two and you were gone with Penny." I cry and go off to the bathroom, Belinda follows me.

"What is your problem, Brina? You can tell me how it was with you and Myles."

"How *what* was?"

"The sex." Belinda whispered. "Everyone knows."

"We didn't have sex. I got messed up on that jungle juice but I didn't have sex with him."

"You told me that you would tell me, no secrets remember?"

"Look, Belinda, I'm still trying to process everything that happened and what didn't happen. But I do know that sex never happened."

"Whatever." Belinda rolls her eyes and starts to leave the bathroom. "Jasper already told me that Myles has your underwear in the locker room. How the hell he even got your drawers is beyond me. But I'm just your best friend! At least I thought I was. Forget it. If you want to be a secret hoe, be undercover about it. I don't need my stock to go down messing with you."

"That's cold, Belinda."

"Listen, if you wanted to shake us at the party to have sex, you could've told me, I would've covered for you."

"I didn't do *anything* and I would believe you if you said the same thing to me."

Belinda shakes her head and leaves.

Tears roll down my face. "*I should've listened to Grandpop about him.*" I wash my face, grab

paper towels and wipe my eyes. I look up.
Penny is standing behind me with a smirk.

"Hey Hoe!" Penny says.

"I'm not a hoe."

"Whatever you say, I don't care. Stay away
from my man. Leaving your drawers in a boy's
room is a thirsty move, Hoe."

"Don't call me a hoe, Penny." I warn her.

Penny rushes forward and pushes me into a
stall door.

"Remember what I said, Hoe."
She quickly leaves.

*"What the heck? Thank goodness it's almost the
end of a Friday. I'm not staying for that last
class with Myles. I'm out."*

I skip class and leave school.
Walking home, I see Yetta's bus.

"I cannot let her see me." I go the back way and go to Miss Mina's house. Before I can knock, Miss Mina says,

"Hey Sweetheart. You're in?"

" I guess I am." She squeals happily and opens the door.

"You're a little early but that's good. C'mon in. I need to get this practice in before Don comes home and wants his dinner." She closes the door. "What can you do?"

"I sing and I can dance a little." I whispered.

"That's great. I was thinking 'The Greatest Love of All' by Whitney Houston."

"I love that song!"

"Good. Come on, I want to see where you are with it."

I begin to sing. I know I'm a little off-key, so I stop.

"Ok, I hear a little something in there, but I know that you can do better. Are you Ok? How was school?

"Nothing. I'm just warming up."

"Well, you were a mess the other night, and you couldn't really talk about then, does any of it have to do with that boy?"

"Miss Mina, I don't want to talk about it. Can we just practice? Please show me the routine."

"Bella, I know that you may not want to talk about it, but I'm here, OK?"

"Yes, Miss Mina."

She looks up at the clock. "Oh! I gotta at least get dinner in the oven. Can you help me so I can move quicker?"

"Sure."

Miss Mina starts to make my favorite. Fried chicken. Feels like I haven't had it in years. When I smell it, my mouth starts to water as I mash the potatoes. When I start to shuck the corn, Miss Mina glances at me and smiles. "You're pretty good at this."

"Of course! I love to cook. I just haven't been in the kitchen in a long time. I used to help my mom all of the time when she was alive."

"Yeah? What did she pass away from?"

"I'm not sure. Grandpop doesn't want to talk to me about it. But I really miss her."

"She sounds like she was a great woman."

"She was. You remind me of her sometimes when you smile and call me Bella. She was so pretty and kind and funny." I start to cry.

"Bella?"

"I'm O.K. I just don't get a chance to talk about her. I just miss her so much. I know that she would fix everything that's wrong in my life."

Miss Mina hugs me. "It's like that sometimes. I didn't know my parents at all. I was raised in the system from birth. Passed around from family to family, don't really know how many times. I ran away when I was 15 and I vowed I'd never go back. Been on my own since. It hasn't been easy, but I made my way. You'll make your way too, Sweetheart."

A car pulls up.

"Don's home. Thank you so much for helping me with dinner. Do you want to stay?"

"MINA! Is my dinner ready?"

An older man storms into the kitchen and stops, startled by Brina's presence.

"Oh, I didn't know you had company."

"Hi Sir, my name is Sabrina, I mean Bella."
I said nervously.

"Well Sabrina, I mean Bella, we have some things to discuss for now so this chit chat with you two has to end."

"I already invited her to dinner, Don. She helped me make it."

"Another time." Don said abruptly.

"It's Ok, Miss Mina. I'll come back for practice tomorrow."

"Bella, I'll save you some chicken. I know it's your favorite."

"Thank you, Miss Mina." I open the screen door.

"Young lady?" Don said. "Thanks for dinner." He slams the door behind me.

I don't know what his problem is. Miss Mina is too pretty for that lunatic anyway. I hope that Belinda isn't right about him hurting her. He seems really mean.

Thank goodness it's Friday. Don't have to see anyone from school.

The next day, Jasper came by the house. I open the door.

"What do you want?"

"I want to say sorry. You're my friend and if what you said is true. I believe you."

"Thank you Jasper. That means a lot to me." I sigh. "And what about Belinda?"

"She's a hard nut to crack. She's just being Belinda. She'll come around."

"Jasper, friends don't say the things that she said to me. I've been through enough for my friends to turn against me too."

"I respect that. And I'm sorry you went through that. Why don't you tell an adult?"

"I'm embarrassed and been shamed enough. People are going to believe what they want about me if I tell the truth or not. I don't want to explain myself to anyone. I'm just tired. There's nothing anyone can do anyway. I just want it all to go away." A tear streams down my face. "I just need a little time, Jasper."

I go into the house. Jasper walks away. I just write everything in my diary. At least I can still tell her everything. My diary doesn't talk back, she just accepts whatever I say, in my voice and I don't have to mince words or omit truths. It is what it is between us. As I write, I fall asleep.

When I wake up, it's already dark. I'm wide-awake. I hear a door slam and I look out of the window.

I see Miss Mina in one of her glittery dresses and her hair down past her waist. Oh, she was breathtaking.

I whisper loudly, "Miss Mina, Can I come? I'll tell Grandpop that we're practicing."

"Oooh yes, I'll introduce you as my daughter as an opening for our entry in the pageant. It'll be good... But... you cannot go with me looking like *that*."

"Looking like *what*?" I look at myself and laugh. Ok. "Let me tell Grandpop I'm going."

"Ok. But hurry! I can't be late."

I tell Grandpop and rush over. When I go into Miss Mina's spare room, it's like a magic show. Dresses everywhere. In order from kind of dress, to color, gowns, short and tall. Shoes on shelves organized the same way. Looked like a museum. My jaw dropped so low, I think I drooled.

Mina laughs. I'm still in awe.
"I don't think that I've ever seen anything like this before."

"How about this one?" She hands me a beautiful dress.

"It's beautiful! For me?"

"Yes, for you. Try it on."

I go behind the screen and the dress went on so effortlessly. I came out and looked in the mirror. I immediately felt beautiful. The dress was emerald green with sequins and when Miss Mina zipped it, it pulled me tight. I had a waist!

"Now look who's breathtaking? Keep it. It's yours."

"Wow!" I smile. "I've never had anything like this."

"Well now you do. Ok. Hair and makeup time."

She grabbed my head and pulled my hair up into a loose bun. Then she did my mascara and added bright red lipstick to my lips. I pursed my lips together before she outlined my lips with a Q-tip. She said that it was for a perfect line on my mouth. I turned around and when I peered into the mirror, I gasped.

"Voila!" She said proudly.

"I feel like a princess!"

We both laughed. When we walked into the club that night, I felt so good about myself. Miss Mina went on stage and performed, I so proud of her. I'm so surprised that she's not famous. This was the best show I've ever seen. I just hope that when it's our turn, I can wow her too.

Compared to last night, Sunday was a humdrum day. As it needed it to be, I was trying to get mentally ready for school. I hated school even more now.

On Monday, Myles had the boys were gawking and whispering while Penny had the girls laughing at me. Belinda and I still aren't talking so being in gym class stunk.

Since I'm on my own now, I signed up for the talent show and practice alone. I decided that I'll sing the song that I'm singing with Miss Mina since I'm practicing it anyway.

The days at school take forever now, with Jasper splitting his time with me and Belinda, still trying to get us to talk. I'll admit that I miss her but I still don't like her right now.

Now I go to Miss Mina's after school to practice and we make our costumes, she gives me advice. We laugh and talk, I always have a good time with her.

One day, she showed me her portfolio of her in magazines.

"Why don't you model anymore?"

"Well, Don likes me at home more. Anyway, I'm not young like I used to be."

She gets up and puts the book away.

She sighs. "But you have what it takes. You're a natural."

"Maybe I will."

Chapter Six
Pageant Day

"**I** couldn't wait to get home from school today. Me and Miss Mina are doing the Mother-Daughter Pageant tonight. I rush home and go straight to her house but Miss Mina isn't answering the door. Maybe she's running errands. So I leave and decide that I'll come back later.

Now it's almost 3 hours till showtime and she's still not answering the door. When I go out back to the back of the house, I see the door is open. I see Miss Mina on the floor, bleeding from her head and legs.

"Miss Mina, wake up! Please wake up! I can't lose you too. Please wake up!" She barely opens her eyes. I call 911 and scream for Grandpop.

When the ambulance comes, she's still in and out of consciousness and I'm so scared for her. I watch the paramedics talk to Grandpop. He's shaking his head and signs some paper. As the ambulance drives away, Grandpop grumbles, "That bastard almost beat her to death."

"Who, Mr. Don?" I ask.

"Whatever *that* man's name is, I'm always praying for that girl, hoping that she'd leave this loser like the last loser. I guess she ain't learned her lesson yet."

After we left Miss Mina's house, it was a quiet night. I was nervous for her and angry with Mr. Don for hurting her like that. I'm confused why someone so beautiful lets someone hurt her. Why doesn't she leave him?

On Sunday, I go up to the hospital to see her and she's still asleep. I sit in the chair and wait. About 45 minutes later, Mr. Don appears. He staring at her and he glances at me.

Normally, I leave when Mr. Don comes around, because I don't like him and he scares me. But this time, I'm not afraid.

I slowly get up and walk towards him, "Why don't you just leave her alone? Don't you want her to be happy? Why would you hurt her like that? What did she do to deserve that from you?"

I start to cry. "Leave or I'm calling the police!"

Mr. Don just stood there for a minute then left the flowers on the chair. As he walked out, he looked at me, almost ashamed. I don't feel sympathy for him. He's a coward.

I take the flowers and throw them in the trash. Miss Mina opens her eyes. Weakly, she says, "Don was here?" I nod. "What did he say?"

"He didn't say anything, just left these." I take the flowers out of the trash.

"Give them to me." She takes them and when she smells them, she musters a painful smile. She catches me cringe.
"He loves me, Bella."

"What? He almost killed you! He beat you and left you for dead!"

"Listen, I don't tell you how to live your life, so don't judge me or Don."

"I don't want to lose you, Miss Mina. You had internal bleeding. Don't you get it? You could've died! That's not love!"

"Don't worry about me. I'm a big girl, Bella. I can take care of myself."

I sit down in amazement and start shaking my head. "I can't believe this. I can't believe this."

"Listen, I'm sorry about the pageant and your $1,000 dollars. We'll have another chance in the future."

"Not if you're dead."

I burst into tears. "I won't watch you die!"

I storm out of the room and out of the hospital. I know that I was harsh but I meant what I said. Thinking about Miss Mina made me scared and sad.

I finally stopped missing my mom so much and thinking of losing Miss Mina makes me feel so lost.

Chapter Seven
Grandpop's Heart

When I got home from the hospital, Grandpop was sitting on the porch in his rocker. "Brina, sit down."

"Yes Grandpop."

Grandpop lifts up my diary. I start to cry. "How did you get it? Did you read it?"

"Yetta found it, I took it before she could get deep into reading it. And yes, I saw some things."

I put my head down.

"I told you not to see that boy anymore."

"Grandpop, I don't want to talk about this."

"Neither do I and I won't pry about it with you right now." Grandpop puts his head down.
"I just don't want you and your cousin to end up like Mina or y'all mothers.

"Our mothers? You care? You never talk about them. So how can we know anything if you never tell us anything? It's not fair."

"Your mother broke my heart, Brina. She went off with that low-down creep, your father and dashed out of town. When he left and she ate herself to death. A damn heart attack at 36! You're not that far away from her, you know."

"Oh you want to talk about my weight now, huh? I'm beautiful, Grandpop. I love myself, weight on, weight off."

"You're killing yourself and I refuse to be a part of it! When your mother died, I lost a huge piece of my heart and here you go, right in her footsteps. Sneaking around with this boy and eating yourself to death! When will *my* heart have a rest? Y'all are killing ME!"

We both got quiet.

A tear went down my cheek. "Do you pray for me, Grandpop?" I asked timidly.

"What?

"You said that you pray for Miss Mina, do you pray for *me*?"

"I know that I don't tell you enough and I promise that I will try harder, but I do love you. And I pray for you all... day... long, *everyday*!" I smile and wipe my eyes.

"Ok. Maybe my approach is wrong."

"Ya think? *Big Bones* is not a nice thing to call someone, Grandpop."

"I'm sorry. I won't do it anymore."

"And tell Yetta to stop."

"O.K., I will." I walk over and hug Grandpop. He continues, "I love you Bella Brina."

I smile. "I love you too, Grandpop."

"Oh, and this business with this boy is not over."

"Yes, Sir".

Chapter Eight
Talent Show

I put on the costume that I was going to wear to the pageant with Miss Mina. Then I put my mascara and lipstick on like she showed me. I hear a car beeping. It's Miss Mina. Putting my head out of the window, Miss Mina shouts, "Please let me take you."

I smile and pop my head back into the window. I grab my purse and walk down the stairs.

Yetta yells, "You look pretty for a..."

Grandpop shoots a sharp look at Yetta that stops her dead in her tracks."

Yetta continues, "You look nice Brina." Grandpop says, "Make sure you save me a seat!"

"Yes Grandpop. One for you and Yetta."

"Me too!" Yetta says.

Me moving towards the door. "Ok. I gotta go, y'all!"

I close the door behind me and Miss Mina has the car running.

"I called a taxi, Miss Mina."

"I sent it away. Please let me take you."

"I have to get my mind right to perform, we can talk later." I start to walk towards the corner towards the cab.

"I left Don, Bella."
I stayed silent.

"I thought about what you said." Miss Mina continues. The cab beeps. "I'll let you go. Can you save me a seat? I'd love to see you perform." I nod my head and get into the cab.

In the car, my head is rushing with all types of thoughts. *"I'm glad that Miss Mina left Don." "The school is still against me." "I hope Grandpop doesn't say anything to Myles." "Calm down Brina."*

I take a deep breath and exhale.
I say aloud, "I got this. I got this."

When I get to the school, it's a mad house! I see all types of acts preparing and let's say that it's gonna be a great show. *Let me save these seats, right now before I forget.* I sip on my water, rest my voice and wait patiently to go on.

Act after act and finally, they call my name.

I step to the microphone to sing and I hear, "Hoe!" the crowd has mixed laughs, another voice sharply, "Shhhhhhh" in the background. I close my eyes and imagine when me and Miss Mina would sing together and I smiled inside.

Then I hear two loud voices in the background over a speaker.

"I should've slutted her out when I had the chance!"
"You mean you didn't sleep with Sabrina?"

"Nah man, she got so messed up on that juice I gave her, she couldn't if she wanted to. So I dick slapped her and took her panties. She literally didn't know what hit her!" He laughs loudly.

"So why did you tell everybody you hit it? It really messed her up."

*"Man, **nobody** ever tells Myles no. Who the hell that fat bitch think she is? Penny got y'all to leave so there would be no interruptions. But no, she just pushed me away and said no, I almost took anyway it but she hit the floor. So I left her there."*

A loud noise sounding like a punch, then a thud, a bang and then a clang.

"Why'd you hit me?"

The recording stops. Dead silence fills the room.

I start crying and ran off the stage.

Belinda is backstage next to the speaker. I run past her. But it's a dead end.

"Don't leave, Brina." Belinda says.

Still crying. "I can't do this. Belinda." I have to get out of here.

"I'm so sorry, Brina. Jasper took the recording and when I heard it, I had to tell everyone."

I'm crying uncontrollably. "But I told you! I told you all."

There's a huge commotion in the auditorium. I look behind the curtain and saw the principal and security are grabbing Myles and Penny and the crowd is booing them.

"Brina, I didn't know what else to do. You deserved justice so I brought it here."

I dried my eyes. "Where's Jasper?"

"He's suspended for fighting Myles. The principal didn't know why they were fighting. All they saw was Myles bloody nose. He really rocked his face!"

After a silence, Belinda and I chuckled.

"You should take your moment. Go ahead and sing, Brina. You're more than everyone thinks and I'm so sorry for not believing you."

"Just so you know, it's not alright between us, Belinda. You really hurt me."

"I know. I'm a jacked up person for that. I just hope one day you'll forgive me."

A teacher comes to the back where we're standing. "Are you OK, Dear?"

"Yes. I'm better Ma'am. Thanks."

"Do you think that you can go on stage and perform?"

"I don't know."

Belinda looks at me. "You got this Girl." She whispered.

Mustering up a smile. "Ok. I'll do it."

I closed my eyes and rocked that song! I mean really rocked it. I sang my heart out so great that Whitney Houston herself would've been proud of me!

When I opened my eyes, I saw Grandpop, Yetta and Miss Mina standing and clapping for me, it felt so good when everyone else got up.

"Encore! Encore!" Someone yelled. "Again, Again!" Someone else screamed. "Sabrina! Sabrina! Sabrina!"

One of the teachers motioned for me to go again. I didn't want to sing anymore but I had to get something off of my chest. When I stepped up again, the crowd hushed.

I closed my eyes and took a deep breath. "Over a month ago, I was assaulted by someone I trusted. Someone you all know." The crowd hummed as I continued. "I have been harassed, embarrassed and shamed ever since. What he tried to take from me no one can take. And I didn't break because I love myself. I always have and I always will. So I am glad that I can entertain you tonight but this is all of the show I have in me. Thank you."

There was a cacophony of disbelief and applause in the crowd as I get off of the stage. I didn't care what anyone thought. I just wanted relief and I got it.

I still don't know how to feel and I definitely can't believe that I just did that. But I did it. I did what I came to do. I put my heart on the stage and 'dropped the mic', so to speak. And I walked out of the school with my head high for the first time in what felt like forever.

I know who I am. I know who I want to be. Nothing can crush me. No one can beat me down.

I love myself. I am strong. I'm Bella.

THANK YOU

This is the first book that I've written with the daughter that I never had in mind. A book that I needed to write so that all of the young girls realize their need to love themselves and know that they are more than enough.

To know that they are precious and have so much to give and are worth so much more than the world can even offer.

Bella Brina has a piece of all of us girls in her. Her experiences, her hopes and dreams and especially her need to be loved.

Thank you for being my inspiration.

You are loved.

About the Author

Birdie Chesson is the Author and Publisher of all of her books. She also teaches others how to write their own books through her coaching workshops and seminars with over 20 years experience as a public figure.
She is the mother of a son, Bam.

To find out more about her, visit:
www.BirdieChesson.com

Are you interested in booking a Workshop, Seminar, Public Appearance or Conference with Birdie Chesson?

Most Popular Workshops:
- Family Talk
- Momtrepreneurs
- Girl Power
- Entrepreneur Love
- Let's Write a Book!

Interested in having Birdie host your next event?

Leave a voice message at 914-933-7433 And/or email Birdie at **BookCoachBirdie@gmail.com**

Thank you for reading a book by:

Please feel free to enjoy her other publications:

- Bam Roberts
- Let's Write a Book
- It's Ok...

And her Children's Books Series'
- Stickboy & Cookie
- "Talk to Me"

**Available on
www.MissBirdiesBooks.com**

www.ingramcontent.com/pod-product-compliance
Lightning Source LLC
Chambersburg PA
CBHW071633040426
42452CB00009B/1601